PEACE CORPS

AGENTS OF GOVERNMENT

TERESA WIMMER

Creative Education • Creative Paperbacks

Published by Creative Education and Creative Paperbacks
P.O. Box 227, Mankato, Minnesota 56002
Creative Education and Creative Paperbacks are
imprints of The Creative Company
www.thecreativecompany.us

Design and production by Chelsey Luther
Art direction by Rita Marshall

Printed in Malaysia

Photographs by Corbis (AP/AP; Bettmann; Corbis; YVES HERMAN/Reuters; Kurdzuk,
Tony/Star Ledger; Wally McNamee; reazsumon/Demotix; Underwood & Underwood), devi-
antART (AllydNYC), Dreamstime (Galyna Andrushko, Demerzel21, Nlphotos, Saiko3p, Ints
Vikmanis), Flickr (Peace Corps), Getty Images (Lyn Alweis, Bill Johnson, New York Daily
News Archive, Lynn Pelham), Newscom (Everett Collection), World University Service of
Canada (WUSC-EUMC)

Library of Congress Cataloging-in-Publication Data
Wimmer, Teresa.
Peace Corps / Teresa Wimmer.
p. cm. — (Agents of government)
Summary: An in-depth look at the people and policies behind the government agency known as
the Peace Corps, from its founding in 1961 to the controversies and challenges it faces today.
Includes bibliographical references and index.

ISBN 978-1-60818-549-8 (hardcover)
ISBN 978-1-62832-150-0 (pbk)
1. Peace Corps (U.S.). 2. Peace Corps (U.S.)—History. I. Title.

HC60.5.W496 2015
361.6—dc23   2014029609

CCSS: RI.5.1, 2, 3, 5, 6, 8; RH.6-8.3, 4, 5, 8

First Edition HC 9 8 7 6 5 4 3 2 1
First Edition PBK 9 8 7 6 5 4 3 2 1

TABLE OF CONTENTS

CHAPTERS

Introduction **4**

Peace Talks **7**

A Tough Job **17**

One Person, One World **27**

New World Issues **37**

AGENCY INSIDERS

At the Beginning **12**

R. Sargent Shriver **22**

Carolyn R. Payton **32**

AmeriCorps **42**

AROUND THE WORLD

Operation Crossroads Africa **15**

Nigeria, 1961 **25**

International Peace Corps **35**

Mondelez Partnership **45**

•

Glossary **46**

Selected Bibliography **47**

Websites **47**

Index **48**

At 2:00 A.M. on October 14, 1960, senator John F. Kennedy delivered a presidential campaign speech to thousands of cheering students

at the University of Michigan. He spoke of starting a volunteer service organization made up of Americans who would travel to underprivileged nations. "How many of you who are going to be doctors are willing to spend your days in Ghana?" Kennedy asked. "Technicians or engineers, how many of you are willing to work in the Foreign Service and spend your lives traveling around the world?" For numerous students—those who heard the speech firsthand and those who didn't—Kennedy's call to action changed their lives. At the time, the world was still reeling from past wars and was on the verge of new conflicts. The idea of using peaceful means to restore relationships between Americans and peoples of other nations was refreshing. In the decades since its founding, the organization eventually known as the Peace Corps has worked to establish bonds of friendship and peace with all its partners and to encourage Americans to gain a better understanding of global societies. Today, the Peace Corps continues to put out the call for volunteers who are ready to change the world.

The youngest person to ever win the White House, John F. Kennedy reached out to America's youth in his speeches.

Peace Talks

The culture of the United States in the 1960s was one of radical change. In the 1950s, many children whose parents had lived through the desperate times of the **Great Depression** enjoyed much more comfortable lives in comparison. However, as these young people neared adulthood in the 1960s, many of them began to see such "comfort" as excess. They reacted against their parents' values and beliefs and searched for another purpose in life. Popular folk singers such as Bob Dylan and Joan Baez expressed the views of this new generation who sought freedom in all its forms.

Young adults of the 1960s did not want to fight in wars like their fathers did. They believed that peace and unity would solve disputes and help people from different cultures understand one other. Civil rights leaders such as Martin Luther King Jr. led peaceful protests to gain equal rights for African Americans. Many young people of all races joined in the fight to achieve basic human rights for everyone in the U.S.

Meanwhile, far beyond America, major changes were taking place. Between 1945 and

The August 1963 March on Washington for Jobs and Freedom gathered more than 200,000 participants in the capital.

1960, many African and Asian countries fought for and won their independence from centuries of European rule. Although these nations had gained equality and the right to govern themselves, they now faced the difficult task of developing new governments. They needed help not only with basic necessities but also with **economic** structure, agriculture, and education. The U.S., as one of the richest and most powerful countries in the postwar era, saw its opportunity to help these **Third World** nations grow and prosper. But citizens of some countries opposed any U.S. involvement. In the late 19th and early 20th centuries, the U.S. had looked to extend its political and economic influence around the globe, particularly in Latin America. Many people criticized these **imperialist** practices and thought the U.S. needed to stop imposing its ideas on others.

After World War II ended in 1945, various members of the U.S. Congress proposed bills to establish volunteer organizations in **developing countries**. In December 1951, Massachusetts representative John F. Kennedy suggested to a congressional group that young college graduates would gain valuable life experience by assisting underprivileged nations. Not long after that, senator Brien McMahon called for young people to act as "missionaries of **democracy**."

The first legislator to propose that a Peace Corps be organized was Minnesota senator Hubert H. Humphrey. In 1957, he introduced a bill to assemble "talented young men and women in an overseas operation for education, health care, vocational [job] training, and community development." However, the proposed law did not meet with much enthusiasm. Many legislators had concerns about sending young Americans to foreign lands, while others believed the idea would simply be impossible to carry out.

In 1959, interest in such an organization grew when Wisconsin representative Henry S. Reuss suggested that a "Point Four Youth Corps" be made up of "young Americans willing to serve their country ... in far-off countries and at a soldier's pay." After returning from a trip to Southeast Asia in 1957, Reuss was determined to change the negative image of the U.S. he had encountered there. In 1960, he and senator Richard L. Neuberger of Oregon introduced companion

> *After World War II ended in 1945, various members of the U.S. Congress proposed bills to establish volunteer organizations ...*

Mahatma Gandhi became famous for his nonviolent resistance of Great Britain's continued rule over India.

As set forth in 1933 by the 20th amendment to the U.S. Constitution, Kennedy was inaugurated on January 20th.

bills in both branches of Congress to link a volunteer corps to the U.S.'s foreign aid program. The bill became law in June, and in August, the Mutual Security Appropriations Act went into effect. It gave $10,000 to the Colorado State University Research Foundation to determine if such a corps would be possible and practical. In February 1961, the foundation issued a report strongly in favor of the youth corps.

When Kennedy campaigned for U.S. president in 1960, he filled many Americans with energy and optimism, especially young people. The idea of a volunteer youth organization became part of the Kennedy campaign's focus on American progress. Kennedy first announced the idea on October 14, 1960, during a late-night speech at Ann Arbor's University of Michigan. He wanted to gauge student interest. The excitement of those 10,000 college students spread to schools throughout the country.

But Kennedy's proposal had its share of critics. Richard Nixon, Kennedy's presidential opponent, believed people would volunteer in order to avoid the draft during wartime. Others doubted that young adults were skilled or mature enough to serve in foreign countries for long periods of time. Kennedy, however, saw a volunteer organization as a way to combat the negative stereotypes of Americans. Many people abroad thought of Americans as loud, arrogant, and ignorant of other cultures because of bad experiences they'd had with such Americans. Kennedy pointed out that the majority of new American Foreign Service officers did not even speak a foreign language. Several U.S. ambassadors had little knowledge of the countries to which they were assigned. Kennedy wanted to demonstrate that Americans were trustworthy, knowledgeable, and compassionate.

Almost 3 weeks after the University of Michigan speech, Kennedy spoke to a crowd of 25,000 at San Francisco's Cow Palace and formally introduced the Peace Corps. "We in the '60s are going to move the world again in the direction of freedom, and I ask your help in doing so," he said.

Kennedy defeated Nixon on November 8 in a close election. During his inaugural address in January 1961, Kennedy famously challenged

Kennedy ... saw a volunteer organization as a way to combat the negative stereotypes of Americans.

Americans to "ask not what your country can do for you—ask what you can do for your country." With that phrase in mind, Kennedy could think of only one person to get the Peace Corps off the ground—his brother-in-law, R. Sargent Shriver. A quiet but energetic man, Shriver was inspired by the work of Catholic social activist Dorothy Day. He once remarked that he asked himself every evening, "What have I done to improve the lot of humanity?"

Shriver was born November 9, 1915, in Westminster, Maryland, and later attended Yale, where he became a founding member of the America First Committee, a **pacifist** group.

However, when the U.S. entered World War II, he served five years in the navy. A religious man devoted to social causes, he became director of both the Catholic Interracial Council (established to mix white and African American schools) and the Chicago Board of Education in 1955. He envisioned the Peace Corps as a large group of young Americans selflessly devoted to serving and improving the lives of those less fortunate abroad.

Shriver's team delivered a report to the president just four weeks after Kennedy's inauguration. The report recommended starting the Peace Corps program immediately. On

AGENCY INSIDER

AT THE BEGINNING

When John F. Kennedy proposed the creation of a peace corps during a 1960 speech at San Francisco's Cow Palace, he was greeted with thunderous applause. "I am convinced," Kennedy said, "that our men and women, dedicated to freedom, are able to be missionaries, not only for freedom and peace, but join in a worldwide struggle against poverty and disease and ignorance." Throughout the country, college students began discussing the idea, and 30,000 Americans wrote to Kennedy in support of it.

Sargent Shriver's friendly and caring personality attracted young followers wherever he traveled around the world.

March 1, 1961, Kennedy signed Executive Order 10924, which officially created the Peace Corps. It defined the Peace Corps as an organization that would "be responsible for the training and service abroad of men and women of the United States in new programs of assistance to nations and areas of the world." Kennedy appointed Shriver as director, and Congress authorized the order on September 22, 1961.

From the beginning, Shriver designed the Peace Corps to be independent of other federal government organizations (despite its belonging to the Department of State) and to have no political agenda. By the summer of 1961, plans for the Peace Corps' structure were laid out. However, the most difficult tasks remained: getting the leaders of Third World countries to allow volunteers past their borders, and then organizing, training, and dispatching those volunteers.

Although President Kennedy envisioned a small Peace Corps, Shriver wanted to start big to take advantage of Americans' enthusiasm for the group. In 1961, polls showed that 70 percent of Americans favored the creation of a Peace Corps. The *Wall Street Journal* was more skeptical, asking how anyone could believe violence in Africa would be helped "because some Harvard boy ... lives in a mud hut and speaks Swahili." Nonetheless, within months of its call for volunteers, Shriver's team had about 11,000 applications from eager young people across the U.S.

President Kennedy welcomed 600-some Peace Corps trainees bound for overseas posts to the White House in August 1962.

OPERATION CROSSROADS AFRICA
New York, New York, U.S.A.

Operation Crossroads Africa (OCA) was acknowledged by President Kennedy to be the model for the Peace Corps. In 1958, Dr. James H. Robinson founded OCA as a program that involved young Americans working alongside local Africans for terms of about six weeks—"building bridges of friendship to Africa" to truly understand another culture. By 2014, more than 11,000 OCA volunteers had served in 40-plus African countries and 12 Caribbean countries.

A Tough Job

With the volunteer applications in place, Shriver's team moved on to gaining support for the Peace Corps abroad. In the spring of 1961, the organizers spent three weeks visiting Africa, Asia, and the Middle East. They asked national leaders to consider accepting volunteers. After Ghana and India accepted, many other Third World nations followed.

To get the new volunteers ready to serve, Shriver's team assigned them to complete 8 or 10 weeks of classroom and field training activities at colleges and other locations across the U.S. and Puerto Rico. Volunteers needed to learn the local language and cultural customs, plus job, agricultural, and survival skills. The first two groups of volunteers left for service in Tanganyika (now Tanzania) and Ghana on August 28, 1961. The 51 members of the Ghana team headed to the capital of Accra to serve as teachers.

Things didn't go perfectly. The volunteers lived at high schools, isolated from the rest of the community, and sometimes had difficulty learning Ghana's Twi language. The **Cold War** climate of the 1960s led some countries, such as the Soviet Union, to accuse the volunteers

Foreign-language training of the 1960s used the audio-lingual method, which emphasized hearing and repeating phrases.

of working as U.S. spies. Still, the volunteers' work was considered successful in Ghana, which faced a lack of schools and teachers. The Ghana Ministry of Education was so pleased that it asked the Peace Corps to increase its number of volunteers to the country.

In the early days of the Peace Corps, its two main programs involved teaching in Africa and community development in Latin America. By December 1961, more than 500 volunteers were serving in such countries as India, Nigeria, Chile, the Philippines, and Pakistan. The following year, 28 additional countries began hosting Peace Corps volunteers, whose ranks had risen to nearly 3,000.

Shortly after the Peace Corps' creation, the Office of Evaluation was established to evaluate the program and the volunteers in each country. Evaluators concluded that the Corps was often unorganized. In some countries, volunteers didn't find out where—or if—they were needed until after they arrived. The evaluators exposed uncoordinated training programs in the U.S. that did not adequately prepare the volunteers for service. In response, the Peace Corps gradually improved its training. It hired former volunteers to staff the training sessions and moved the training overseas after a brief orientation period. Peace Corps officials also attempted to improve volunteers' teaching methods by encouraging them to spend time in their students' communities.

When President Kennedy was assassinated on November 22, 1963, people around the world mourned. At the same time, the U.S. was becoming more involved in the Vietnam War, which began in 1955. Young Americans were spurred by a desire to continue Kennedy's dream and to make a difference in a war-weary world. In 1966, the Corps reached an all-time high of 15,556 volunteers, with programs in 55 countries. To make sure that Peace Corps staff remained fresh, a rule was established in August 1965 that limited most employees to five years of service. Shriver resigned as director the following year to devote himself to other **humanitarian** organizations.

By the mid-1960s, the U.S. was sending more and more troops to the Vietnam War, but the conflict became increasingly unpopular among young people. As the U.S. sent thousands more troops to Vietnam, many young Americans took to the streets in protest. And many others who

> *Young Americans were spurred by a desire to continue Kennedy's dream and to make a difference …*

Protests against the Vietnam War spread into Canada by the late 1970s, as neighboring citizens also opposed U.S. action.

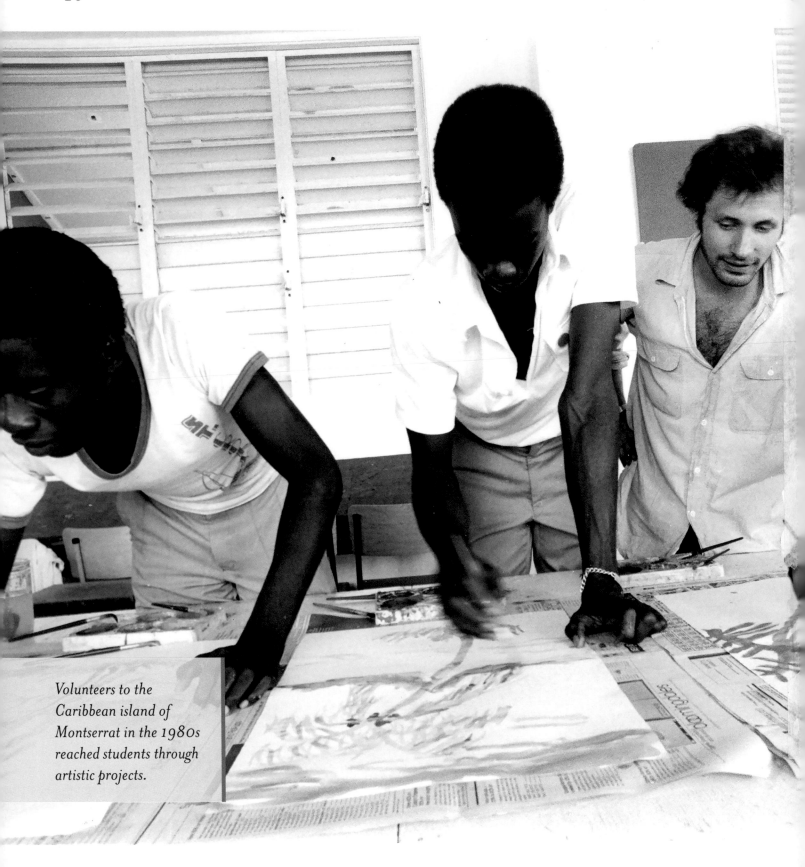

Volunteers to the Caribbean island of Montserrat in the 1980s reached students through artistic projects.

would have volunteered for the Peace Corps protested the war by *not* joining the Corps. They did not want to be associated with any program of the U.S. federal government. Other young men were drafted to serve in Vietnam. As a result, Peace Corps applications dropped from 42,000 in 1966 to 14,000 by 1977.

In 1969, Peace Corps director Joseph Blatchford called for the organization to recruit volunteers who were older, more mature, and more highly skilled. He opened up the application process to married couples with children and focused on recruiting **minorities**. More changes came on July 1, 1971, when President Nixon issued an executive order that folded the Peace Corps and several other service programs into a new federal volunteer agency called ACTION.

Peace Corps officials did not welcome the reorganization. When Richard F. Celeste became director in 1979, he demanded that the Peace Corps regain its **autonomy**. President Jimmy Carter then signed an executive order that gave the Peace Corps control over its own activities. It regained full independence from ACTION in 1981.

Although the Corps' ranks continued to decline into the 1980s, the smaller numbers seemed to work in the organization's favor. Volunteers were better trained in languages, cultural differences, and job skills than those of the early days. But they also often experienced more loneliness and poverty. In 1989, director Paul D. Coverdell changed the name of the organization to the U.S. Peace Corps despite the objections of many government officials. Because Corps volunteers worked as private citizens (and not as part of the U.S. government), officials were concerned the name change would be misleading. As a result, the name was officially changed back to Peace Corps in 1992.

When the Soviet Union collapsed in 1991 and the formerly **communist** countries of Eastern Europe opened to Westerners, the Peace Corps benefited. Countries such as Poland, Hungary, and the Czech Republic asked for Peace Corps volunteers to assist with social and economic programs. This sent Peace Corps officials into a frenzy to get new volunteers in place.

Although the Corps' ranks continued to decline into the 1980s, the smaller numbers seemed to work in the organization's favor.

Most of the volunteers in Eastern Europe taught English or helped to develop small businesses. In doing so, they reintroduced **capitalism** to nations that had long lacked free markets. The hurried nature of the operations, however, led to many of the same problems the Peace Corps had encountered in its early days: insufficient volunteer training, a lack of qualified training staff, and underdeveloped projects. Sending volunteers to these countries also forced budgets to be cut for existing Peace Corps programs in Africa, Asia, and Latin America—which, in turn, caused strain within the organization itself. Furthermore, some Americans began to question the Peace Corps' motives for sending volunteers into European countries where the majority of citizens were already literate and skilled.

Budget cuts in the 1990s forced U.S. officials to re-examine the Peace Corps program. Officials decided to again concentrate their efforts on helping African, Latin American, and Southeast Asian countries. By 2002, volunteers had left all the countries of Eastern Europe and the former Soviet Union, except for those where conditions remained unstable. Carol Bellamy, who became Peace Corps director in 1993, was the first former volunteer to lead the organization. Her term set off a string of former volunteers serving as director.

AGENCY INSIDER

R. SARGENT SHRIVER

After resigning as Peace Corps director in 1966, R. Sargent Shriver continued to help those less fortunate. As director of the Office of Economic Opportunity under president Lyndon B. Johnson, Shriver helped to design the war on poverty, which aimed to assist poor people and ethnic minorities. He founded the Sargent Shriver National Center on Poverty Law in Chicago in 1967 and later served on the board of the Special Olympics. In 1994, Shriver received the Presidential Medal of Freedom.

More than a decade after volunteering in Guatemala, Carol Bellamy became president of the New York City Council.

In 1996, in an attempt to expand Peace Corps activities, director Mark Gearan created the Crisis Corps. The Crisis Corps was a program that assigned former Peace Corps volunteers to temporarily serve areas around the world that had been hit by disasters. In 2004, a tsunami ravaged the Southeast Asian countries bordering the Indian Ocean. The Crisis Corps sent volunteers to help construct water treatment plants and assist people who had lost their homes. The Crisis Corps also sent 272 former Peace Corps volunteers to the U.S. Gulf Coast in 2005 after Hurricanes Katrina and Rita flooded thousands of homes and businesses. In 2007, Peace Corps director Ron Tschetter changed the name of the Crisis Corps to the Peace Corps Response.

In the first decade of the 21st century, many members of the U.S. Congress, other government officials, business leaders, and teachers counted themselves among the ranks of former Peace Corps volunteers. When president Barack Obama took office in 2009, he pledged to increase the funding and size of the Peace Corps. However, an economic downturn that forced budget cuts across the board put that idea on hold. Despite its limited budget, the Peace Corps continued in its successful missions of helping those in need.

The December 2004 tsunami that struck Southeast Asia left millions in need of food, shelter, and medicine.

NIGERIA, 1961
Africa

In October 1961, a postcard written by Margery Michelmore, a Peace Corps volunteer in Nigeria, was found by Nigerian college students. In the postcard—which Michelmore had intended to mail to her boyfriend in the U.S.—she described Nigeria's "primitive living conditions." Her remarks insulted the local community and prompted many Nigerians to de

One Person, One World

Throughout its more than 50-year history, the Peace Corps' scope and leaders have changed, but it has remained an important U.S. institution. To carry out its mission of peace and friendship between nations, it relies on its most important asset: its people. Between 1961 and 2014, more than 215,000 volunteers served in the Peace Corps. Those volunteers, along with agency officials, have worked together to make the Peace Corps a leader in international goodwill throughout 139 countries.

To help keep those volunteers informed, the Peace Corps publishes a quarterly newsletter, the *Peace Corps Times*, which is distributed to all volunteers in the field. The newsletter provides Peace Corps-related news from across the globe and allows volunteers to share information on their successful projects with fellow volunteers.

The Peace Corps is an independent agency within the executive branch of the U.S. government. The U.S. president appoints the Peace Corps director and deputy director, and the U.S. Senate must confirm the appointments. The director is advised by the heads of other offices

No matter the political climate between countries, overseas volunteers focus on the people they came to serve.

such as the General Counsel, Victim Advocacy, Congressional Relations, and Innovation. The Office of the Inspector General (OIG) is an independent office within the Peace Corps and reports directly to the director and Congress. The OIG evaluates the Peace Corps continually, advising the director on ways to prevent fraud, waste, and mismanagement within the program.

In June 2014, Carrie Hessler-Radelet became the 19th director of the Peace Corps. She was a former Corps volunteer, having served in Western Samoa from 1981 to 1983. As deputy director in 2010, she led the rollout of the Focus In/ Train Up program, which provided volunteers with more specialized technical training and online learning communities for current volunteers, staff, experts, and returned volunteers to discuss ideas. She also helped to create the Office of Global Health and HIV and the Global Health Service Partnership.

The Senate Committee on Foreign Relations and House Committee on Foreign Affairs oversee the activities and programs of the Peace Corps. Congress determines the Peace Corps' annual budget. Generally, the Peace Corps budget represents about 1 percent of the foreign operations budget. Although the Peace Corps budget has fluctuated throughout the years, it grew from $30 million in 1961 to $356.3 million in 2013.

The agency consists of two main areas: overseas posts and headquarters offices. Posts are organized into three regions: Africa; Europe, the Mediterranean, and Asia; and Inter-America and Pacific. At each post, American and host country professionals oversee the volunteer activities in the local communities. As of 2014, the Peace Corps had active programs in 65 countries that were administered through overseas posts. Each post was managed by a country director. Support staff included safety and security, medical, programming, financial, training, and administrative workers.

The Paul D. Coverdell Peace Corps Headquarters in Washington, D.C., coordinates the general operations of the agency. Its purpose is to support the overseas posts and ensure the safety and security of volunteers. The agency currently employs about 1,100 staff members, including headquarters staff, those at regional offices, and overseas staff. Among other activities, headquarters staff develops, monitors, and evaluates programs and develops training standards. Regional directors at headquarters manage

> *The agency consists of two main areas: overseas posts and headquarters offices.*

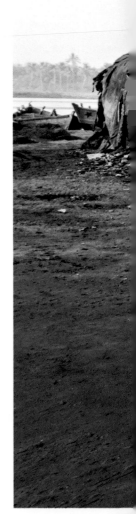

Volunteers may encounter desperate living conditions while on assignment— even in Goa, India's richest state.

Agricultural or environ-mental knowledge informs volunteers who construct irrigation systems in erosion-prone areas.

volunteer efforts, coordinated through the Office of Global Operations. The headquarters staff is also responsible for convincing skilled and energetic Americans to join the Peace Corps. Regional recruiting offices exist across the country. Along with field-based recruiters located in several cities and on college campuses, they work to recruit Americans for Peace Corps service.

In a typical year, roughly 15,000 apply for about 4,000 available Peace Corps positions. Ninety percent of volunteer positions require a bachelor's degree—favored applicants have a degree in agriculture, forestry, or a related environmental field and are skilled in Spanish or French. However, certain positions accept appropriate work experience in place of a degree. Specialists such as urban planners, engineers, and university-level professors are also in high demand. Applicants with a leadership and community service background are also more likely to be chosen. Anyone can request a particular country assignment, but no guarantees are made. Generally, applicants will be matched with available open positions based on their

background field and skills. They are placed in the areas of education, youth in development, health, community economic development, agriculture, and environment. After a candidate submits an application and health history form, a recruiter reviews the application and interviews the candidate, nominating successful candidates for acceptance. Applicants then must pass legal clearance and match an open position before receiving an invitation to join the Peace Corps. The more flexible applicants are about where they will be placed and when they can leave for duty, the more likely they are to be chosen.

In addition to a three-month training period, most Peace Corps volunteers serve abroad for two-year terms. However, volunteers can ask to have their term of service extended. All volunteers must be U.S. citizens of at least 18 years of age. In 2013, 7,209 volunteers served in 65 countries worldwide. They assisted with programs involving education, health, environment, community economic development, and agricultural services.

There are also specialized programs within the Peace Corps. The Global Health Service

Generally, applicants will be matched with available open positions based on their background field and skills.

Partnership is a Peace Corps program that places nurses and physicians in medical and nursing schools abroad for a period of one year. They help train medical personnel and improve healthcare in developing countries. The Peace Corps Response is composed of returned volunteers and other professionals with at least 10 years' work experience. They serve for 3 to 12 months to provide targeted, short-term assistance in places where they are needed most. The Peace Corps has also involved itself in the education of its volunteers. Through Master's International, volunteers can incorporate their Peace Corps service into their master's degree pro-

gram. In addition, the Paul D. Coverdell Fellows Program provides graduate school scholarships to volunteers after they return from service.

The life of a Peace Corps volunteer is not glamorous. When the volunteers sign up for service, they receive a stipend (a set amount of money) to cover such basic necessities as food, housing, and local transportation. The amount varies from country to country, but each volunteer receives an amount that allows him or her to live at the same level as the local people they serve. In addition, the agency provides two vacation days for every month of service, and volunteers can travel home to visit family or

AGENCY INSIDER

CAROLYN R. PAYTON

In 1977, Carolyn R. Payton became the first woman and African American to hold the position of Peace Corps director. After earning a PhD in counseling and student administration from Columbia in 1962, Payton was appointed Peace Corps director for the Eastern Caribbean region in 1966. As one of only two female country directors, her success was critical in proving that women could effectively do the job, paving the way for other women and minorities to take leadership roles within the agency.

In West Africa's Niger, traditional homes in rural areas are made of mud brick and topped with a thatched roof.

receive family while serving overseas. When a volunteer's tour of duty ends, he or she receives a "readjustment allowance" of about $8,775.

Volunteer conditions vary greatly depending on the site. Volunteers at one location may have an apartment in the city, while volunteers at another may live in a hut. Others live with local families. Some might not even have running water or electricity. In 2014, 46 percent of Peace Corps volunteers were on assignment in Africa. The region with the next largest percentage of volunteers was Latin America (20 percent), followed by Eastern Europe/Central Asia (13 percent). The remaining volunteers served in various other regions around the globe.

Because of its widespread reach, the Peace Corps regularly receives more requests for new country programs and additional volunteers than can be met with available funding. However, the federal government's refocus on expanding the Peace Corps in the early 21st century paid off. In 2010, the number of volunteers reached a 40-year high of 8,655 Americans. Peace Corps volunteers reflected the diverse population of the U.S.: The average age of a volunteer was 28; 7 percent of volunteers were over the age of 50; and the oldest active volunteer was 86. Nineteen percent of volunteers were minorities, while 60 percent were women.

Annual flooding in countries such as Cambodia makes it necessary for houses and other buildings to be raised on stilts.

INTERNATIONAL PEACE CORPS
Ottawa, Ontario, Canada

Many countries worldwide have volunteer service organizations similar to the Peace Corps. The World University Service of Canada (WUSC) and its sub-programs offer Canadians the opportunity to serve and study overseas. WUSC's Uniterra program is Canada's largest international volunteer program,

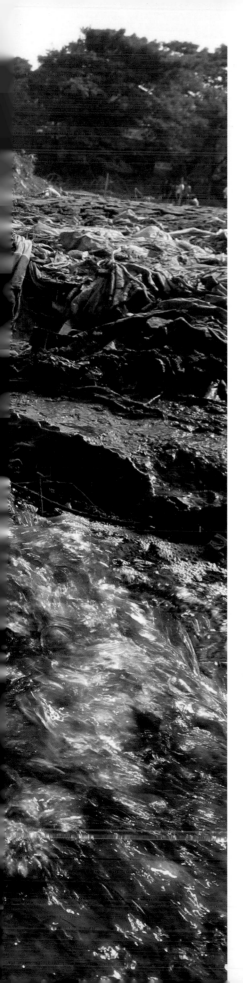

New World Issues

In the 21st century, Peace Corps volunteers in Third World countries battled many of the same issues of the past. Countries still faced poverty and lack of sufficient food and drinking water, and they still called upon volunteers to help improve those conditions. But there were plenty of new challenges, too. The rise of environmental awareness worldwide led volunteers to tackle environmental issues, such as soil erosion, during their time abroad. They taught communities better farming methods that would not deplete natural resources. They helped local farmers learn about **composting** and safe ways to control pests. Peace Corps volunteers also instructed local people, businesses, and schools about climate change and recycling.

Agriculture is one of the largest employment sectors in most developing countries served by the Peace Corps. To help ensure food security worldwide, the U.S. government instituted the Feed the Future program. Partnering with the U.S. Agency for International Development (USAID), Peace Corps volunteers have introduced new ways for local people to grow

Severely polluted rivers in Third World nations present health hazards and obstacles to transportation and trade.

their own food, address water shortages, and feed their families.

The resurgence of old diseases and the rise of new ones also challenged Peace Corps staff. For centuries, malaria, a flulike illness that is spread by mosquitoes, killed millions of people in tropical countries. However, efforts in the 20th century by health-service organizations such as the Peace Corps led to the disease's elimination in 108 nations.

Unfortunately, progress in malaria control was hampered—and in some cases, reversed—by program funding cuts beginning in 2008. This led to a resurgence of the disease in some countries, especially in South Africa. Through the Peace Corps' Stomping Out Malaria in Africa program (launched in 2011), more than 3,000 Peace Corps volunteers traveled throughout Africa to assist with the treatment and prevention of malaria. Volunteers also partnered with international teams for the program Malaria No More.

In 1981, a new disease called Acquired Immune Deficiency Syndrome, or AIDS, was first diagnosed in humans. Thought to originate in Africa, the disease spread quickly and claimed the lives of millions of people worldwide. Even though no known cure exists, medical advancements have made great strides in treating AIDS and HIV (the virus that causes AIDS). The Peace Corps partnered with the President's Emergency Plan for AIDS Relief (PEPFAR), which provides assistance to countries most affected by the HIV/AIDS epidemic. Today, the Peace Corps trains all volunteers who serve in Africa, the Caribbean, Eastern Europe, and Central Asia to be educators of HIV/AIDS prevention and care.

Volunteers use today's technology—cell phones, the Internet, and social media—to make a difference in the communities in which they work. In 2013, Peace Corps volunteers in countries such as Rwanda organized information and communications technology camps to teach female high school students computer skills.

> *Volunteers use today's technology ... to make a difference in the communities in which they work.*

Peace Corps volunteers in Cameroon worked with their local communities to improve high school computer labs. Technology also helps volunteers in education, the Peace Corps' largest program area. Volunteers work in schools as math, science, English, and resource teachers. They also develop libraries and technology resource centers for communities.

Senegal's management of HIV/AIDs involves hospitals providing healthy foods for their patients, with volunteer help.

The largely agricultural country of Benin in West Africa supports a population of nearly 10 million.

In recent years, the Peace Corps has strengthened its partnerships with other national and independent organizations, from USAID to the Millennium Challenge Corporation. It also looked for ways to work with United Nations agencies on training and other collaborative efforts. In 2011, the agency undertook a new initiative to create partnerships with federal organizations such as the Environmental Protection Agency as well as leading nongovernmental organizations such as Mercy Corps.

In coming years, the Peace Corps will need to adapt its response to a constantly changing world. Peace Corps officials must continually monitor the political climate of other nations to ensure the safety of volunteers as well as to look for new opportunities to serve. But critics have accused Corps officials of not doing enough to protect its volunteers. From 1991 to 2000, major physical assaults to volunteers more than doubled (from 8 to 17 per 1,000). Some have accused the agency of failing to ensure that all houses supplied by foreign governments are secure before assigning volunteers there. In addition, volunteers are often deployed to areas with limited access to police or medical services.

The dangers volunteers face range from nonviolent property crimes (such as theft) to serious crimes, including assault, rape, and murder. Between 1961 and 2013, 294 volunteers died while serving in the Peace Corps. Although most deaths were accidental, others resulted from in-country violence or violence at the hands of fellow volunteers. In 2009, 24-year-old Kate Puzey was murdered while volunteering in Benin, allegedly by a fellow Peace Corps volunteer. The agency was accused of mishandling events before and after Puzey's murder. "The Peace Corps has done its best to keep word of the case and its apparent mistakes quiet," said ABC News. In 2011, President Obama signed the Kate Puzey Peace Corps Volunteer Protection Act. The act imposed new policies and practices to reduce the risks for volunteers and to make sure Peace Corps officials respond effectively and compassionately when crimes do occur.

Along with other reforms, the Peace Corps formally launched the Sexual Assault Risk

... officials must continually monitor the political climate of other nations to ensure the safety of volunteers ...

Reduction and Response program in September 2013. It included more than 30 policy changes; extensive sexual assault response training for both volunteers and staff; and new procedures for reducing the risk of sexual assault. Despite an increase in crime among volunteers throughout the past five decades, a 2008 survey of former volunteers showed that 92 percent felt safe where they lived and volunteered.

Since the agency's founding, critics have accused the federal government of using the Peace Corps for its own military gains. They say the federal government plays upon the agency's goodwill to win other nations' support for U.S. military actions. To help avoid potential conflicts, former members of the Peace Corps cannot be assigned to military intelligence duties for four years following their Peace Corps service. They are also prohibited from ever serving in a military intelligence position in countries where they volunteered.

In 2014, perhaps the biggest challenge facing the Peace Corps was how to balance an increased need for volunteers with limited funds. Aaron Williams, the Peace Corps' director from 2009 to 2012, stated that countries and communities wanted more volunteers than the agency had the resources to provide. Beginning in 2010, President

AGENCY INSIDER

AMERICORPS

The Peace Corps has helped inspire service programs within America's borders. Founded in 1994, AmeriCorps is a service program made up of 80,000 Americans each year. They serve at nonprofits, schools, public agencies, and community groups across the country. Volunteers serve for terms of 10 months to 1 year. They also receive health coverage, training, and, upon the completion of their assignment, an education award to be used for college or the repayment of student loans.

Director Williams and then senator John Kerry appeared at a Global Health Service Partnership event in 2012.

Obama's call to service inspired a number of Americans to consider Peace Corps service. In response, the agency began to focus on balanced growth in order to make sure volunteers had good experiences.

Some people wonder if the Peace Corps is still needed. Thanks in part to the agency's volunteers, education and communications systems in developing countries have also greatly improved since the 1960s, causing some to say the agency's job may be done. The number of people attending college in Panama—a popular Peace Corps destination—has risen from 7 percent in the 1960s to 45 percent today. But a 2011 Peace Corps survey found that only 44 percent of people in host countries believed that Americans outside the Corps were committed to helping them.

Critics point out that other programs provide similar services as the Peace Corps at a fraction of the cost to the federal government. They cite the Fulbright Program, which awards grants to American students, teachers, and professionals to study, teach, and conduct research in more than 155 countries. For each Fulbright recipient, the federal government pays $32,000 per year—about $20,000 less than it spends on each Peace Corps volunteer.

Peace Corps volunteers strive to become global citizens—to have an understanding of the rest of the world in order to be more effective in their careers and lives. Although the Peace Corps has experienced many changes throughout the years, its dedication to serving underprivileged people worldwide remains as strong as ever. Indeed, many call it "the toughest job you'll ever love."

Since 1963, more than 2,300 Peace Corps volunteers have bonded with residents of Central America's Panama.

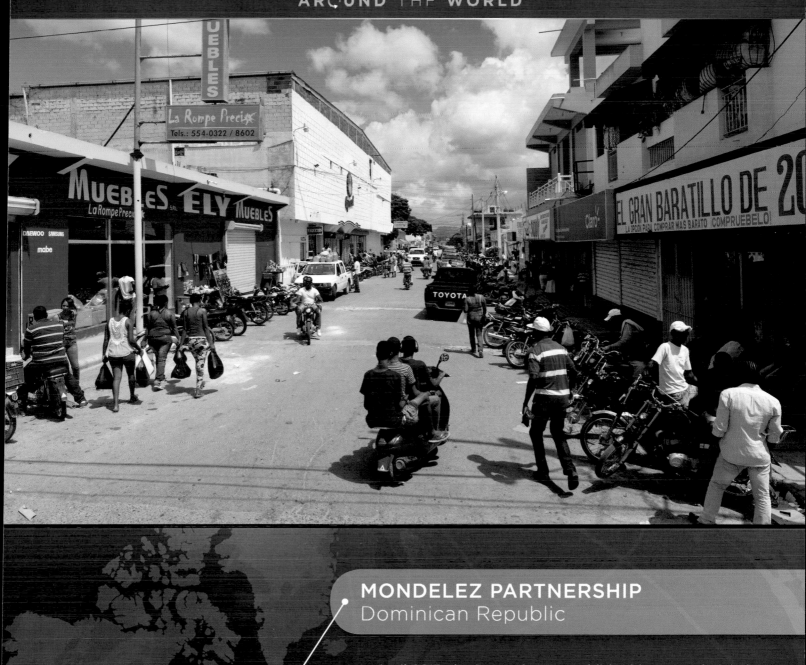

MONDELEZ PARTNERSHIP
Dominican Republic

In April 2013, the Peace Corps established its second global partnership with a corporation, Mondelez International (formerly Kraft Foods), to support agriculture and community development. Mondelez provided resources, and the Peace Corps provided volunteers. The partnership created the "Build Your Dreams" program in the Dominican Republic for

GLOSSARY

autonomy independence or freedom; the right to self-government

capitalism an economic system in which investment in and ownership of the production, distribution, and exchange of wealth is made by private individuals or corporations, instead of cooperatively or by the government

Cold War a period of rivalry after World War II between the communist Soviet Union and the democratic United States

communist having to do with belief in a governmental system in which all property is owned by the community as a whole

composting collecting decaying organic matter, such as from leaves and manure, to improve soil structure and provide nutrients

democracy a form of government in which the people hold power, exercised either directly or through elected representatives

developing countries the poorest nations, which are generally characterized by a lack of healthcare, nutrition, education, and industry; most developing countries are in Africa, Asia, and Latin America

economic having to do with the system through which goods are produced, distributed, and consumed

entrepreneurship starting, organizing, and managing a new business

Great Depression the period of terrible worldwide economic conditions that began in 1929 and lasted throughout most of the 1930s

humanitarian concerned with improving the welfare or happiness of people

imperialist the policy of a nation extending its rule or authority over foreign countries, or of acquiring and holding colonies and dependencies

minorities groups of people who differ from the majority and are often discriminated against

pacifist someone who believes that violence of any kind is unjustifiable and that one should not participate in war

Third World the underdeveloped countries of Africa, Asia, and Latin America; the term was first used during the Cold War to describe the nations that did not align themselves with the policies of either the U.S. or the Soviet Union

SELECTED BIBLIOGRAPHY

Banerjee, Dillon. *The Insider's Guide to the Peace Corps: What to Know Before You Go*. 2nd ed. Berkeley, Calif.: Ten Speed, 2009.

Cobbs Hoffman, Elizabeth. *All You Need Is Love: The Peace Corps and the Spirit of the 1960s*. Cambridge, Mass.: Harvard University Press, 1998.

Hill, Kerry G. "Interview with Peace Corps Director and UW Alum Aaron S. Williams." *University of Wisconsin—Madison Division of International Studies*. April 12, 2011. http://international.wisc.edu/blog/index.php/2011/04/12/interview-with-peace-corps-director-and-uw-alum-aaron-s-williams-2/.

Lihosit, Lawrence F. *Peace Corps Chronology: 1961–2010*. 2nd ed. Bloomington, Ind.: iUniverse, 2011.

Meisler, Stanley. *When the World Calls: The Inside Story of the Peace Corps and Its First Fifty Years*. Boston: Beacon, 2011.

Peace Corps. "Homepage." http://www.peacecorps.gov/.

WEBSITES

Habitat for Humanity
http://www.habitat.org/youthprograms/ages_9_13/ages_9_13_default.aspx
Learn about Habitat for Humanity youth programs and how you can make a difference.

Peace Corps for Kids
http://www.peacecorps.gov/kids/
Explore the globe as a Peace Corps volunteer in this interactive game challenge.

Note: Every effort has been made to ensure that the websites listed above are suitable for children, that they have educational value, and that they contain no inappropriate material. However, because of the nature of the Internet, it is impossible to guarantee that these sites will remain active indefinitely or that their contents will not be altered.

INDEX

African countries 4, 8, 14, 15, 17, 18, 22, 25, 34, 35, 38, 41

AmeriCorps 42

Asian countries 8, 17, 18, 22, 24, 28, 34, 35, 38

Canada 35

  Students Without Borders 35

  World University Service of 35

Caribbean 15, 32, 38, 45

Carter, Jimmy 21

cultural values of the 1960s 7, 18, 21

European countries 21, 22, 34, 38

Foreign Service 4, 11

Fulbright Program 44

Johnson, Lyndon B. 22

Kennedy, John F. 4, 8, 11–12, 18

King, Martin Luther Jr. 7

Latin American countries 8, 18, 22, 34, 35

Michelmore, Margery 25

Millennium Challenge Corporation 41

Mondelez International 45

Nixon, Richard 11, 21

Obama, Barack 24, 41, 44

Paul D. Coverdell Peace Corps Headquarters 28

Peace Corps directors 12, 14, 17, 18, 21, 22, 24, 27, 28, 32, 42

  Bellamy, Carol 22

  Blatchford, Joseph 21

  Celeste, Richard F. 21

  Coverdell, Paul D. 21, 28

  Gearan, Mark 24

  Hessler-Radelet, Carrie 28

  Payton, Carolyn R. 32

  Shriver, R. Sargent 12, 14, 17, 18, 22

  Tschetter, Ron 24

  Williams, Aaron 42

Peace Corps organization 4, 8, 11, 12, 14, 17, 18, 21, 22, 24, 27–28, 31, 32, 34, 37, 41–42, 44, 45

  budgets 22, 24, 28, 42

  country directors 28, 32

  founding 4, 12, 14, 42

  headquarters offices 27–28, 31

  legislative lead-up 8, 11

  name changes 21

  overseas posts 28

  overseen by Department of State 14

  presidential appointments 27

  purposes 4, 27

  reforms of 41–42

  regional offices 28, 31

  support staff 28

  volunteers 14, 17, 18, 21, 22, 27, 28, 31, 32, 34, 37, 41, 44, 45

  within ACTION 21

Peace Corps projects and programs 17, 18, 21, 22, 24, 28, 31–32, 37–38, 41, 42, 45

  AIDS education 38

  Build Your Dreams 45

  Congressional oversight 28

  and dangers involved 41, 42

  environmental awareness 37

  Focus In/Train Up 28

  Global Health Service Partnership 28, 31–32

  malaria elimination efforts 38

  natural disaster response 24

  and Office of Evaluation 18

  and Office of Global Operations 31

  opportunities for returned volunteers 32

  recruiters 31

  training for 17, 18, 21, 22, 28, 31, 41

President's Emergency Plan for AIDS Relief 38

Puzey, Kate 41

Robinson, James H. 15

  and Operation Crossroads Africa 15

Soviet Union 17, 21, 22

  and Cold War 17

U.S. Agency for International Development (USAID) 37, 41

Vietnam War 18, 21

World War II 8, 12